Becoming an Evocative Coach

Becoming an Evocative Coach

A Practice Guide for the Study of Evocative Coaching and Evoking Greatness

Jeanie Cash

Donnita Davis-Perry

George Manthey

For information:

Corwin

A SAGE Company

2455 Teller Road

Thousand Oaks, California 91320

(800) 233-9936

Fax: (800) 417-2466

www.corwin.com

SAGE Ltd.

1 Oliver's Yard

55 City Road

London EC1Y 1SP

United Kingdom

SAGE Publications India Pvt. Ltd.

B 1/I 1 Mohan Cooperative Industrial Area

Mathura Road, New Delhi 110 044

India

SAGE Publications Asia-Pacific Pte. Ltd.

18 Cross Street #10-10/11/12

China Square Central

Singapore 048423

ISBN: 978-1-0718-2014-8

Program Director and Publisher: Dan Alpert

Senior Content Development Editor: Lucas Schleicher

Copy Editor: Christobel Colleen Hopman

Typesetter: TNQ Technologies

Proofreader: Benny Willy Stephen

Indexer: TNQ Technologies

Cover Designer: Candice Harman

Marketing Manager: Sharon Pendergast

20 21 22 23 24 10 9 8 7 6 5 4 3 2 1

Table of Contents

With love and heartfelt thanks, this guide is dedicated to Bob and Megan Tschannen-Moran, the creators of the evocative coaching process. Their books Evocative Coaching *and* Evoking Greatness *provide a structure for listening, empathizing, appreciating, and designing in a way that impacts those being coached as well as the coach. We cherish our relationships with Bob and Megan as we are grateful for the expanding network of evocative coaching relationships that not only improve learning and teaching but also transform lives—one conversation at a time.*

About the Authors

Jeanie Cash is the Co-founder of Lead Learner Associates. She retired as the Assistant Superintendent of Educational Services in the Placentia-Yorba Linda Unified School District in Southern California after 33 years in education. She taught elementary and middle school and served as a principal for 14 years. For 13 years, Jeanie was the Assistant Superintendent of Educational Services for two large suburban districts in Southern California. She serves as a coach and consultant for both the Association of California School Administrators (ACSA) and for Leadership Associates. Jeanie has had several articles published on leadership. She coaches both district and site leaders and provides leadership development training throughout California. Jeanie is the past-president of ACSA's State Council for Curriculum, Instruction, and Accountability. She led ACSA's Southern California Academy for Curriculum and Instructional Leaders for several years. For the past 28 summers, she has been a team leader and coach for ACSA administrative training programs at UCLA. Jeanie's leadership has been frequently honored. Examples include, the Curriculum and Instruction Leader of the Year for ACSA Region 17 in Orange County (2011), The CASCD Helen Heffernan Outstanding Educational Leader Award (2006), and NAESP saluted her as a National Distinguished Principal in Washington D.C. (1997). She earned her M.A. from the University of La Verne.

Donnita Davis-Perry joined the Virginia Department of Education (VDOE) Training and Technical Assistance Center (T/TAC) at the College of William and Mary in 2002, with 30+ years of experience as a general and special educator. At T/TAC, Donni provides professional learning sessions and follow-along coaching to support educators to full implementation of evidence-based practices. Donni has expertise as an Instructional Consultation Team (ICT) facilitator and coaches new ICT members to enhance, improve, and increase student and staff performance nationwide. Donni has multiple coaching certifications and is the lead certifier for Evocative Coaches at the Center for School

Transformation and Lead Learner Associates. Donni's areas of expertise include assistance with instructional and leadership coaching, student progress monitoring, formative assessment, learning strategies, inclusive practices, providing specially designed instruction to students with disabilities, project-based learning, and co-teacher collaboration. She earned a M.Ed. in Education from Old Dominion University.

George Manthey is the Co-founder of Lead Learner Associates. He retired as the Assistant Executive Director, Educational Services, of the Association of California School Administrators (ACSA) after 40 years in education. He taught elementary school as a regular classroom teacher and taught both elementary and middle school students as a special day class teacher and resource specialist. He was an elementary school principal for 10 years in the San Francisco Bay Area. George served as Assistant Executive Director of ACSA from 2006 to 2013, responsible for all of ACSA's educational programs and conferences. In addition to his work with Lead Learner Associates, George serves as the Program Co-coordinator for all educational credential coaches in the ACSA program in the Silicon Valley. George has received a number of awards including the Whitney Foundation Award for Outstanding Contributions to Education (1984) and the California Association of Supervision and Curriculum Development's highest honor—the Helen Heffernan Award for Outstanding Instructional Leadership (2012). He has written over 60 columns for *Leadership* magazine as well as numerous articles that have been published in *Leadership, the School Administrator, Learning Environments Research Journal,* and *Educational Leadership.* George earned his Ed.D. from the University of California, Santa Cruz.

Foreword

As educators begin to sharpen their focus on equipping students with deeper learning and thinking skills, school leaders and teachers need support as they change and refine their professional practice. Research has demonstrated again and again that coaching is by far the most effective means for bringing about swift, robust, and lasting change. This practice guide is designed as a companion text to both *Evocative Coaching* and *Evoking Greatness*; the former geared toward coaches who support the work of teachers, while the latter is geared toward those who support educational leaders at the school and district levels. The intended learning outcomes for this practice guide are to master key elements of the evocative coaching model in order to host engaging and inspiring coaching conversations that contribute in meaningful ways to the improvement of the professional practice of teachers and leaders. With strong reliance on strengths-based theory and evidence-based practice, this guide will assist you to develop your knowledge and skills as a coach. You will be inspired and assisted to practice the evocative coaching model, framed around the acronym LEAD: **L**isten, **E**mpathize, **A**ppreciate, and **D**esign.

First, you will attend to your coaching presence, meaning the kind of energy you bring to a coaching conversation. You will learn how to convey a sense of calm assurance and an openness to possibility, as well as a sense of playfulness or lightheartedness to enhance the creativity of you and your coaching partner. You will then work to hone your listening skills. Almost everyone recognizes the importance of good listening to successful coaching and successful relationships in general. And most of us probably think that we are already pretty good listeners. That is, until a conflict centered around a misunderstanding arises, or we get feedback suggesting that our communication partner doesn't feel heard. Exercises in this guide will help you to build your listening and empathy skills so that you better forge a strong working alliance with your coaching partner before you ask them to take the kinds of risks that change entails.

Adopting an appreciative, strengths-based approach to coaching may sound like a great idea, until you try to put it into practice. It is all well and good when we are working with a highly skilled educator, but it can seem counterintuitive when we are working with someone who is struggling. And yet, building self-efficacy is important to fostering the motivation to experiment with new practices and to persist in the face of setbacks. Finally, design thinking has come to the forefront in many educational circles, but not necessarily as a process to assist educators to improve their practice. Evocative coaching is a design thinking process that brings a clear, coherent structure to coaching conversations, leading to the development of SMARTER experiments, and to debriefing those experiments once they have taken place. This practice guide enhances self-reflection with activities designed to provide guided practice in the skills described, in order to continuously improve your coaching practice. The activities in the practice guide do not repeat the information in the text—they expand on them by inviting both reflection and practice of the model. With the exercises in this practice guide, the skills of evocative coaching will begin to come more naturally as they more and more come to characterize your coaching practice.

It has been astonishing how deeply the core principles of the evocative coaching model have resonated with people throughout the world. One of the most delightful things to come out of publishing both *Evocative Coaching* and *Evoking Greatness* has been the wonderful people it has brought us into relationships with, and the three people who authored this practice guide are at the top of that list! Jeanie and George both hail from California, Jeanie in Southern California and George from Northern California. After retiring from outstanding careers as educators and educational leaders at the classroom, school, district, and state levels, they joined forces to create Lead Learner Associates to support the work of educators through coaching and consulting. They had dreamed of writing a book one day to capture their accumulated wisdom and to offer a positively oriented coaching model for working with educators. But when George read *Evocative Coaching*, he called Jeanie to exclaim, "Somebody wrote our book!" Together, they have offered face-to-face and distance training in evocative coaching throughout California, across the United States, and internationally.

Donni and I have been colleagues at the William & Mary School of Education for nearly two decades, but we didn't know each other until 2009 when *Evocative Coaching* brought us together. Although Donni holds certifications in a number of coaching models, the underlying principles and message of evocative coaching resonated deeply with her, as it had with Jeanie and George. It affirmed the knowledge that she had accumulated over a long career as a general and special educator, as well as in her work supporting educators to enact evidence-based practices to enhance student and staff performance here in Virginia and nationwide. Donni has a particular passion for supporting educators who work with students with special needs and those who live in challenging circumstances. To the work of writing this practice guide, she brings long experience as the lead certifier for evocative coaches at the Center for School Transformation and Lead Learner Associates.

In this practice guide, Jeanie, Donni, and George offer ready access to the exercises and activities they use in their trainings to anyone who wants to deepen their understanding and use of the evocative coaching model. This practice guide may enhance the learning of people encountering the evocative coaching model through face-to-face or distance trainings, through trainings conducted within a school district, an intermediate unit, or a professional association, of a group of colleagues engaged in a book study of either book, or those working on their own. The activities in this guide have been used in the on-site training of cooperating teachers who are preparing to host student teachers in their classrooms, as well as for university supervisors who oversee student teachers. These activities have also been useful in the preparation of school leaders for their instructional leadership and supervisory roles and for the professional development of practicing school leaders as they retool their skills to foster greater innovation among the teachers of their school. The evocative coaching method has proven to be an effective way to engage with novice, mid-career, and veteran teachers and educational leaders alike. We hope that you will enjoy the explorations ahead on your journey!

In addition to the tools and activities in this guide, we invite you to visit the Center for School Transformation website at www.schooltransformation.com for additional resources.

—Professor Megan Tschannen-Moran

William & Mary School of Education

Preface

> If you want to improve, "get a coach." "If you want to be great, you need a great coach."

The wisdom of these words has been well accepted in athletic circles for generations. Only in the last decade or so has this wisdom come to be accepted in the educational realm. To achieve outstanding results in learning and teaching, coaching matters! Leaders lead *people* and it is the people that get results. Teachers teach *students* and it is the success of students that matters most. You can have an admirable vision, hire the right people, and yet not achieve the desired results. Having a coach can improve the likelihood of success.

How does coaching help? With a coach, people learn to listen to one another, express empathy, appreciate through inquiry, and design new ways of being. Not only can they achieve their desired results—they can do so with exhilaration and excitement.

For far too long, improvement efforts in education have been based on a deficit model. Auditors, evaluators, and consultants have gone into schools and districts to determine the reasons for the achievement gap and have left lengthy reports to identify areas for improvement. These reports were all focused on "what's wrong." Strengths-based coaching, the foundation of the evocative coaching model, is a game changer! Neuroscience has demonstrated that people thrive when there is hope—when they have the opportunity to utilize their strengths and focus their attention on what's *right*, rather than what's *wrong*!

In our experiences in training coaches at all levels, we have seen dramatic changes in the emotional and educational climate. As schools and school systems focus on equipping students with deeper learning and 21st century skills, this shift requires that teachers and leaders be supported in changing and growing their instructional and leadership practices. Research has demonstrated time and time again that coaching is by far the most effective means for bringing about swift, robust, and lasting change. The evocative coaching model has proven to be a powerful and compelling model. All professional athletes and musicians will testify to the fact that a coach helped them on their journey to greatness. They would also say it takes practice! The dance of using the four movements of evocative coaching—to *listen, empathize, appreciate*, and *design*—takes practice.

This practice guide is designed as a companion text to both *Evocative Coaching* and *Evoking Greatness*. The guide captures the activities used in evocative coaching workshops and is meant to accompany the text rather than serve as a replacement.

Who might use this practice guide?

- Participants in an evocative coaching workshop, either in face-to-face, hybrid, or distance formats
- A Professional Learning Community or group of educators engaged in a book study of either book
- Any pair, trio, or small group of professionals who wish to expand their coaching skills through the processes of evocative coaching
- Someone wanting to engage in self-study (a partner will be needed for many of the activities)

Since the publication of the first edition of *Evocative Coaching*, the *Center for School Transformation* and *Lead Learner Associates* have provided both online and in-person workshops in which participants have the opportunity to practice the techniques and principles of evocative coaching. The authors of this practice guide, all of whom have taught evocative coaching in multiple settings, have also practiced these strategies in their own leadership coaching. We have been transformed by the evocative coaching model. It is our hope that the readers of this guide will experience a similar transformation as they begin the lifelong journey of using evocative coaching to make a difference and provide life-giving support to those they coach.

If you want to be great, get a great coach! If you want to become a great coach, we hope you discover the "how" in this practice guide.

NOTES for using this guide:

Becoming an Evocative Coach has been organized to correspond to the chapters of *Evocative Coaching* (Tschannen-Moran & Tschannen-Moran, 2020) and *Evoking Greatness* (Tschannen-Moran & Tschannen-Moran, 2018). Both of these texts provide a thorough explanation of the evocative coaching process. The major difference between the two books is that the scenarios provided in *Evocative Coaching* share experiences coaching teachers, whereas the scenarios in *Evoking Greatness* reference coaching leaders.

The activities in *Becoming an Evocative Coach* should be completed after reading, reviewing, and reflecting on either the *Evocative Coaching* or *Evoking Greatness* texts. Space for writing is provided after a brief introduction to the activity—each connected to the techniques and philosophy of evocative coaching. For those who would prefer to complete the activities using a digital device, electronic copies are available at leadlearner.org/becoming-an-evocative-coach-resources. To the left of the open space for writing, the authors have made comments or asked questions as if we were whispering in the reader's ear as the activity is completed. We hope they provide you with a sense that we are by your side as you are *becoming an evocative coach*.

The No-Fault Turn

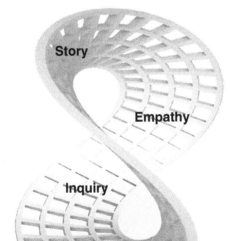

The Strengths-Building Turn

The Möbius Model of Evocative Coaching

Acknowledgments

Thank you to Bob and Megan Tschannen-Moran for entrusting us to take the lead in sharing the evocative coaching model locally and internationally. A special thank you to Margaret Arthofer, Tracy Robinson, and the Association of California School Administrators for believing in us and enabling us to train hundreds of leadership coaches to work with new and aspiring school leaders to obtain their clear administrative credentials.

We would also like to acknowledge both online instructors and those who gave their time to review this practice guide: Jeanie Cockell, Lisa Emerson, Susan Jones, Butler Knight, Shelley Littleton, Sara Miller, Susan McDonald, and Kathleen Pietrasanta.

A special thank you to Maura Rawn, Chief Operations Officer for the Center for School Transformation, for her support and organizational savviness.

Thank you to my husband, Ron, for his love and support with the many hours I'm away from home to coach and to train coaches. To Abigail, Esther, Madison, Sarah, Mackenzie, Sam, and Judah—you inspire me to keep a'goin! JC.

To Liam, thank you for being my partner on the path. DDP.

Someday we'll arrive at that far shore, at a place "discovered, not evoked." Laura, thanks for being on that journey with me. GM.

Practice for an Introduction to Evocative Coaching

1

Evocative coaching is "the calling forth of motivation and movement in people, through conversation and a way of being, so they achieve desired outcomes and enhance their quality of life." (Tschannen-Moran & Tschannen-Moran, 2018, p. 22).

To accomplish that, evocative coaching takes a person-centered, no-fault, strengths-based approach. Coaching becomes evocative when coaches assist coachees through

- Eliciting emotions

- Finding one's voice

- Moving people toward their desired destination.

The principles and practices of evocative coaching are anchored in adult learning theory and growth-fostering psychologies. Whether or not we have formally studied those theories, our own experiences often reveal many of the same principles.

Activity 1.1 Interview

To explore your own experiences and beliefs, conduct an **interview** with a friend or colleague. Ask them to tell you about an experience that they had of learning as an adult that they found particularly meaningful and engaging.

What about that learning experience made it so fruitful and enlivening? How does that experience continue to impact the ways you work with others?

_____

Activity 1.2 Adult Learning Reflection

Reflect on what was shared.

What characteristics were shared that particularly facilitated adult learning?

_____

Activity 1.3 Adult Learning Characteristics

Further reflect on what was shared, especially aspects that included the characteristics of adult learning.

People are inherently creative and capable.

_____

_____

_____

_____

_____

_____

_____

_____

The human brain enjoys novelty and growth.

_____

_____

_____

_____

_____

_____

Challenges can be reframed as opportunities to learn and grow.

_____

_____

_____

_____

_____

_____

_____

_____

How were these characteristics of adult learning present in the story you heard?

Coaches or mentors (or friends) can inspire and challenge us to go beyond what we would do on our own.

_____

_____

_____

_____

_____

_____

_____

////////////////////////////
How were these characteristics of adult learning present in the story you heard?

Empathy, mutuality, and connection make people more cooperative and open people to change.

_____

_____

_____

_____

_____

_____

Evocative coaches navigate the coaching process ever aware of five animating coaching concerns. These are

- **Consciousness**—a desire for increased self-awareness, self-knowledge, and self-monitoring; mindfulness

- **Connection**—establishing a life-giving connection; dialogue

- **Competence**—a belief that coachees are whole, creative, resourceful, and resilient already; a desire to discover, recognize, and celebrate competency

- **Creativity**—creating a "no-fault" playground; adopting a beginner's mind; brainstorming; curiosity; win-learn equation

- **Contribution**—building self-efficacy; reconnection with the coachee's desire to contribute to the learning and growth of students, families, and communities

These concerns are woven into the professional learning relationship evocative coaches are building with teachers and school leaders. It's the quality of the relationship between you and the person you are coaching that, more than anything else, generates the desired outcome; this is the bottom line of coaching presence.

Activity 1.4 Coaching Demonstration

Listen to a coaching demonstration between Bob Tschannen-Moran and Lynn, https://youtu.be/DMjvdo5EhLM. Reflect on the initial question Bob asked of Lynn, "What are some strategies, or movements, that you want to learn that will help you be a masterful coach?" Then describe how the five coaching concerns showed up in the conversation.

Consciousness

_____

_____

_____

_____

Try to recall the words Bob used that reflected each coaching concern.

Connection

_____

_____

_____

_____

Competence

_____

_____

_____

_____

Listen for how Bob demonstrated each of the concerns.

Creativity

_____

_____

_____

_____

_____

_____

_____

_____

_____

Contribution

_____

_____

_____

_____

_____

In addition to the Five Concerns, the coaching conversation also included the four steps of the evocative coaching process: listening, empathizing, asking, and designing.

Activity 1.5 Coaching Demonstration for LEAD

Either through recalling the conversation and/or playing it again, identify the parts of the conversation where you noticed each of the four steps of evocative coaching.

Jot down the phrases that you heard which connected to each step of the evocative coaching process.

Listening

_____

_____

_____

_____

_____

_____

Empathizing

_____

_____

_____

_____

_____

_____

_____

Asking

_____

_____

_____

_____

_____

_____

_____

_____

_____

Jot down the phrases that you heard which connected to each step of the evocative coaching process.

Designing

_____

_____

_____

_____

_____

_____

_____

_____

_____

_____

Activity 1.6 Coaching Platform

Write a coaching platform that puts into words your hopes and intentions as a coach. A coaching platform states clearly and concisely how you understand the purpose of coaching as well as how you frame your aspirations and view your possibilities for fulfilling that purpose. Our coaching platforms are dynamic wishes for how we intended to show up for our coachees. They evolve over time as we do and can be reimagined often.

///////////////////////////
What are the basic values, beliefs, and ethical standards that will inform your coaching practice? How do you hope to enhance the professional development of those with whom you work?

_____

_____

_____

_____

_____

_____

_____

_____

_____

_____

_____

_____

_____

_____

_____

_____

_____

_____

///////////////////////////
What will you do to become the coach you just described?

_____

_____

_____

_____

_____

_____

_____

_____

_____

_____

_____

Practice for Coaching Presence 2

//

Evocative coaching includes two turns, the *No-Fault Turn* and the *Strengths-Building Turn*. The *No-Fault Turn* provides an opportunity to establish our coaching presence. If we skip or rush through this turn, we'll likely create resistance. The *No-Fault Turn* seeks release, relief, ease, and openness to change. The key to coaching presence is to "come alongside" and connect respectfully with those we are coaching (rather than pushing, pulling, or correcting them). If we push people in the direction we want them to go, we provoke resistance and undermine the coaching relationship.

Coach as Whisperer: Much can be learned about coaching presence from Monty Roberts (2000), a world-famous horse trainer who helped to revolutionize the ways horses are understood, approached, and trained.

Activity 2.1 Coach as Whisperer

Watch these two videos of Monty Roberts and reflect on how they apply to coaching.

- *Cruelty is Not Needed—https://www.youtube.com/watch?v=A0P7yXu2-mI*

- *Join-Up Example—https://www.youtube.com/watch?v=9Dx91mH2v00*

///////////////////////////

In what ways are our coachees "roped" into doing things in a certain way, against their will? In what ways may they feel troubled or trapped?

_____
_____
_____
_____
_____
_____
_____
_____
_____
_____
_____
_____
_____
_____
_____
_____

///////////////////////////

What did you sense when the horse lowered its head, came in, and offered itself to Monty, the moment of "Join Up?" How does Monty's energy reflect the kind of energy in coaching that builds trust?

_____
_____
_____
_____
_____
_____
_____
_____
_____
_____
_____
_____

Another way to understand the process of "Join Up," especially when it comes to joining up with people rather than horses, is to rely upon the research and writing that Megan Tschannen-Moran and her colleagues have done regarding trust in teaching and school leadership. Review her definition and discussion of trust in Chapter 2 (*Evocative Coaching*, pages 33–39 *or Evoking Greatness*, pages 26–31). "Trust is the willingness to be vulnerable to another based upon the confidence that the other is benevolent, honest, open, reliable, and competent" (Tschannen-Moran & Hoy, 1997). When these facets are present, the coaching space becomes an inviting and generative platform for learning, growth, and change.

Activity 2.2 Exploring Trust

Consider a high trust relationship you have with someone. How do the five facets of trust show up in that relationship?

Benevolence

_____

_____

_____

_____

_____

_____

_____

How do you recognize each facet? How do you convey it?

Honesty

_____

_____

_____

_____

_____

_____

Openness

_____

_____

_____

_____

————————————————————————

————————————————————————

Reliability

————————————————————————

————————————————————————

————————————————————————

————————————————————————

————————————————————————

/////////////////////////////
*What might be
the result if any
one of these
characteristics
was not
present?*

Competence

————————————————————————

————————————————————————

————————————————————————

————————————————————————

————————————————————————

————————————————————————

————————————————————————

————————————————————————

————————————————————————

————————————————————————

————————————————————————

————————————————————————

————————————————————————

————————————————————————

The key to coaching presence is to "come alongside" and respectfully connect with the teachers or school leaders we are working with rather than to push, pull, or correct them. The way we "show up" for our coachees impacts our ability to support them and how they trust us. Being mindful about our practice connects us and helps build trust with our partners in meaningful ways.

Brainstorming: Generate ideas for developing coaching presence and creating energy check-ins. Remember we evoke ideas during our brainstorm when we

- Don't judge as ideas come forth

- Go for quantity rather than quality

- Share wild and crazy ideas!

- Look for ways to continue and expand ideas

Activity 2.3 Brainstorming

Brainstorm ideas and share with others to generate a massive list. Brainstorm the practices that assist you to get into "a coaching frame of mind" before a coaching session.

Follow the rules of brainstorming. Generate as many ideas as you can. Don't censor yourself!

_____

_____

_____

_____

_____

_____

_____

_____

_____

_____

_____

_____

_____

_____

_____

_____

_____

Oftentimes, beginning evocative coaching sessions with a creative energy check-in is the first signal to our coachees that something interesting is about to happen, and that this won't be a run-of-the-mill conversation. Inviting our coachees to check in with themselves on where their energy is and what's pressing for them connects them to what they want to focus on. Coaches can masterfully weave their coachees' check-in throughout the conversation, using their own metaphors to support their understanding of their needs. Coaches conclude their sessions by checking in again to confirm what's improved and nudge coachees to continue to pay attention to what's on their hearts.

Activity 2.4 Creative Energy Check-In

Brainstorm **creative Energy Check-Ins** to use to begin your evocative coaching conversations. Get creative, unleash the fun!

Examples of creative Energy Check-Ins:

Create your own list of creative Energy Check-Ins. Use one to begin your next coaching session.

- What school supply item do you need in your backpack of resources that will assist you in a successful start to the school year?

- What type of candy bar most represents your emotions about starting this new coaching session?

- I am thinking about when we were kids and the ice cream truck came to our neighborhood, what cool treat most represents our work as we move forward?

_____

_____

_____

_____

_____

_____

_____

_____

_____

_____

_____

_____

_____

_____

_____

_____

_____

_____

_____

As evocative coaches we show up to serve. We listen to our coachees' stories and empathize with them in ways that encourage them to feel heard. We suspended our own ideas, beliefs, and values so that we can be fully present to their experience.

Activity 2.5 Reflection Without Judgment

Reflect, discuss, or journal on creating judgment-free coaching.

How is a judgment-free environment important to our coaching conversations?

_____

_____

_____

_____

_____

_____

_____

_____

_____

_____

_____

_____

_____

_____

_____

_____

_____

_____

_____

_____

_____

_____

_____

Evocative coaches understand the importance of developing trust to fully support our coachees. The five facets of trust represent a combination of intention and attention that opens up the people we are coaching to the possibility of change. The bottom line: where there is no trust there is no way for coaching to be evocative.

How do the five facets of trust play out, or not, in that relationship?

Remember: Trust is not earned once and for all. It is earned, or lost, during every moment of every coaching conversation.

Activity 2.6 Importance of Trust

What is the nature of the interdependence and vulnerability between coaches and coachees?

With a learning partner reflect on a difficult professional relationship (peer-to-peer, coaching, supervising, being supervised) and how and where the facets of trust showed up in that relationship.

Benevolence

_____

_____

_____

_____

_____

_____

_____

_____

Honesty

_____

_____

_____

_____

_____

_____

_____

_____

_____

_____

_____

How do the five facets of trust play out, or not, in that relationship?

Openness

_____

_____

_____

_____

_____

_____

_____

_____

_____

_____

_____

Reliability

_____

_____

_____

_____

_____

_____

_____

What is the nature of the inter-dependence or vulnerability between coaches and coachees?

Competence

/////////////////////////////
What was the result if any of the five facets was not present?

_____

_____

_____

_____

_____

_____

_____

_____

_____

_____

_____

_____

_____

_____

_____

_____

_____

_____

_____

_____

_____

_____

_____

_____

_____

_____

_____

_____

_____

_____

_____

Productive coaching spaces are life-giving spaces marked by three energies:

1. Calm Assurance—"My certainty is greater than your doubt."

    a. If we don't believe that the teacher or school leader we are coaching has the potential to grow, we probably aren't the right coach for them

    b. Don't catastrophize when our coachees are frantic

    c. Embody ease

2. Lightheartedness, what Bob Tschannen-Moran calls playfulness—The work is serious business, but that doesn't mean we have to be serious all the time

    a. We can laugh at situations and ourselves

    b. This unleashes creativity and imagination

    c. Have fun

3. Openness to Possibility—Expect wonderful surprises and good things to happen

    a. Navigate by curiosity

    b. You will see what you believe

    c. Be adventurous

Activity 2.7 Coaching Energies

With a partner, explore the final aspect of coaching presence, holding the coaching space. Ask your partner, "What is one thing in the realm of self-care that you have been longing for but putting off?" After careful listening, the coach intentionally conveys one of the three coaching energies in a response.

_____

_____

_____

_____

_____

Which energy did you select? Share any insights that sparked new possibilities.

_____

_____

_____

_____

_____

_____

//////////////////////////////
*Reflect and
journal on
what was
learned.*

_____

_____

_____

_____

_____

_____

_____

_____

_____

_____

_____

_____

_____

Evocative coaches tune their ears to stories by listening for where the energy and excitement are occurring. We reflect on what we've heard by pointing them to what needs are valuable to them and how they were met or unmet in their story. This experience evokes ease and openness for change.

Activity 2.8 Coaching Practice

Interview someone about a lesson learned during their first year of teaching, leading, or other professional practice. Use an energy check-in. As you listen be judgment-free. Build trust. Be aware of all the energies of coaching presence.

_____

_____

_____

_____

_____

_____

_____

_____

_____

What did you discover in your session about your coaching?

_____

_____

_____

_____

_____

_____

_____

_____

_____

_____

_____

Activity 2.9 Coaching Presence

Review the coaching platform you developed in the last chapter. Reflect on what your coaching platform means to you and how it influences your coaching presence.

_____

_____

What does your platform convey about your coaching presence?

_____

_____

_____

_____

_____

////////////////////////////

How does it represent your intention in creating coaching spaces for the energies of calm assurance, light-heartedness, and openness to possibility?

_____

_____

_____

_____

_____

_____

_____

_____

_____

_____

_____

_____

_____

_____

_____

_____

_____

_____

_____

_____

_____

_____

_____

_____

_____

_____

_____

_____

_____

Practice for Listening for Stories

3

///

As coaches, the value we bring to the coaching relationship starts with creating the space for teachers and school leaders to tell their stories. When we are really listening to a person, we are communicating: "I hear you, I'm here for you, and I believe in you. I'm receiving the gift of your story and I'm holding it as a sacred trust."

In many ways story listening is an intuitive process that can provide us with answers and insights because when we get the people we are coaching to tell us their stories with feeling then they are able to communicate beyond the surface storyline of the story.

Activity 3.1 Mindful Listening

Ask someone, a family member, friend, or colleague, to tell you about a time when they felt challenged. Listen openly and practice "mining for the good."

_____

_____

_____

_____

_____

_____

_____

_____

What did you hear? How did sharing your insights on the positive impact your coachee?

_____

_____

_____

_____

_____

_____

_____

_____

_____

Remember: Hidden in the word LISTEN is the word SILENT. Rearrange the letters again and you get ENLIST. That's the power of Quiet Listening.

Activity 3.2 Story Listening

John Maeda is a world-renowned artist, graphic designer, computer scientist, and educator whose career reflects his philosophy of humanizing technology. For more than a decade, he has worked to integrate technology, education, and the arts into a 21st-century synthesis of creativity and innovation. "Although there have been many proponents of changing STEM to STEAM to incorporate the arts, the movement has been largely championed by John Maeda" (Gunn, 2020). Browse to the following URL and hear John describe how important it is for leaders to LISTEN as opposed to TELL.

https://www.youtube.com/watch?v=U8-Q70gV2Yk&t=28s.

What did you hear John say would be the advantages of a leader "listening" rather than "telling."

_____

_____

_____

_____

_____

_____

_____

_____

_____   *What did John*

_____   *say about*

_____   *empathy?*

_____

_____

_____

_____

_____

_____

_____

_____

_____

_____

_____

_____

_____

_____

_____

Activity 3.3 Quiet Listening

This activity requires a partner. "Person A" will be the person doing the talking. "Person A" will talk for five minutes without interruption. They can talk about anything that is alive for them right now, about how they are showing up today, about a situation they are puzzling over, or a decision they are trying to make. It's like unraveling a ball of string—where it goes doesn't matter. If they run out of things to say before the time is up, they may remain in silence until they think of something more they'd like to say or until the time is up.

The role of "Person B" is to listen attentively, mindfully, and quietly. This means that "Person B" will not speak, ask questions, or respond verbally for those five minutes; "Person B" will be silent. Don't take notes, just listen with your full attention.

At the end of five minutes, "Person B" will reflect what they heard from "Person A." After that round, the two of you will switch roles and "Person B" will be the one talking for 5 minutes. "Person A" will listen and not respond until the end of 5 minutes. "Person A" will then reflect what they heard.

How did it feel to be the person being listened to for five minutes? How was it to listen silently to someone for five minutes?

_____

_____

_____

_____

_____

_____

_____

_____

_____

_____

_____

_____

_____

_____

_____

_____

_____

_____

_____

_____

Activity 3.4 Reflective Listening

Evocative coaches are encouraged to take a "WAIT and SEE" attitude during coaching conversations. We say WAIT: Why Am I Talking? And then SEE: Stop Explaining Everything (Stevens, 2008, p. 163).

1. Interview a person about a lesson learned during their first year of teaching or other professional practice.

2. Request permission to audio record the interview. Listen to the recording and reflect on yourself as a listener.

What were the high points and challenges of listening to their story?

After reflection on the session, what might you do or say differently? How might that change the experience and learning for your coachee?

By inviting our coachees to explore their stories from different angles, we assist them to reframe their experience, to take control of it, and to deepen the understanding of what is really going on.

Activity 3.5 Imaginative Listening

After reviewing pages 68–73 in *Evocative Coaching* or pages 63–66 in *Evoking Greatness* find a partner and have them tell you about a thrilling or challenging experience. Have the partner retell the story using imaginative listening techniques: vantage points, pivot points, and/or lesson points. Respond to the questions below.

In what ways did this approach to story listening release new possibilities?

What insights or "ah-ha's" emerged?

Practice for Empathize for Connection

4

///

Expressing empathy is about validation. How do teachers and school leaders feel when they get done talking with us? Do they feel heard? Do they know they matter? Do they have a sense that their needs are recognized, respected, and valued? Do they feel understood and accepted? Parker Palmer puts this beautifully when he wrote: "We must remember this simple truth: the human soul does not want to be fixed, it wants simply to be seen and heard" (Palmer, 1998, p. 156).

When people feel heard, they open up and become ready to talk about what's next and what's possible. All people want to feel heard and accepted. Feeling heard and accepted will help create their readiness to move to action orientation of the Strengths-Building Turn.

Activity 4.1 Observations Without Evaluation

Practice making **observations** rather than **evaluations**.

Example:

Evaluation: *That kid is a stupid, lazy, and foul-mouthed pain-in-the-neck.*

Observation: *When you gave directions he repeated what you said in a way that resulted in the other students laughing.*

Evaluation: *My principal is never around when needed.*

Observation:

_____

_____

_____

_____

_____

_____

///////////////////////////////
Turn each of
these
evaluative
statements
into an
observation.

Evaluation: *The problem with these kids is their parents.*

Observation:

_____

_____

_____

_____

_____

_____

Turn an evaluation you have heard into an observation.

Evaluation heard:

_____

_____

_____

Observation:

_____

_____

_____

_____

_____

Activity 4.2 Distinguishing Feelings From Thoughts

Practice distinguishing feelings from thoughts. Turn each of these "thought" statements into an observation of a feeling.

Example:

Thought: *I feel that she is being so rude.*

Feeling: *I'm guessing you might be feeling irritated or annoyed.*

Thought: *I'm feeling pressured by my boss.*

Feeling:

_____

_____

_____

_____

_____

_____

Thought: *I'm never able to get through to her.*

Feeling:

_____

_____

_____

_____

_____

_____

Words selected from Figure 4.4 (pages 97 and 98) in Evocative Coaching *or Figure 4.4 (pages 88 and 89) in* Evoking Greatness *will be helpful with this activity.*

Turn a "thought" you have heard into a feeling.

Thought heard:

_____

_____

_____

Feeling:

_____

_____

_____

_____

_____

_____

Activity 4.3 Distinguishing Between Needs and Strategies

Practice distinguishing between needs and strategies. Identifying as accurately as possible the underlying needs that are driving behavior is at the heart of expressing empathy.

Example:

Strategy: *I've got to get these people to listen to me.*

Need: *I'm guessing that your needs for respect, appreciation, and safety are really strong right now.*

Strategy: *There has to be more time for collaboration.*

Need:

_____

_____

_____

_____

_____

Turn each of these strategy ideas into a suggested need.

Strategy: *We've got to do a better job of using direct instruction at this school.*

Need:

_____

_____

_____

_____

Turn a strategy you have heard into a need.

Observations Strategy heard:

_____

_____

_____

_____

Need:

_____

_____

_____

_____

_____

_____

Activity 4.4 Feelings and Needs

Find a friend who will describe for you a hard-to-hear message that they either received or delivered lately. It can be either personal or professional.

Feelings

_____

_____

_____

_____

_____

_____

_____

_____

_____

Needs

_____

_____

_____

_____

_____

_____

_____

As you listen to a hard-to-hear story refer to the chart in this chapter titled, Reframing Causal Attributions (pages 97–98) in Evocative Coaching *or Reframing Faux Feelings (pages 88-89) in* Evoking Greatness. *Write the words that best capture both the feelings (from Column Two) and the needs (from Column Three) that were expressed.*

_____

_____

_____

_____

After listening, share the feelings and needs words you selected with your partner. Remember to suggest the feelings and needs rather than state what you believe they are. It's a stronger expression of empathy when you strive for clarity by saying, "It sounds like you might be boxed in, which could make you wish for some autonomy," rather than being evaluative by expressing, "Wow! You were boxed in there and what you need is to have some choice."

Sympathy Versus Empathy

Often sympathy and empathy are confused and one is substituted for the other. Merriam-Webster defines sympathy as "an affinity, association, or relationship between persons or things wherein whatever affects one similarly affects the other." Empathy is defined as "the action of understanding, being aware of, being sensitive to, the feelings, thoughts, and experience of another." The distinction is important. When we are sympathetic we go down the same path as another. We experience emotional contagion. When we are empathetic, we communicate that we understand that path.

Expressing empathy can feel stilted until you have practiced enough so that the words flow smoothly. The following activity is designed to help you understand and be familiar with the essential parts of an empathetic statement. Once the distinctions are clear in your mind you won't use these stems, necessarily, when expressing empathy, but you will understand the necessary "ingredients."

Activity 4.5 Empathy Statements

Use the Reframing Causal Attributions chart (pages 97–98 in _Evocative Coaching_) or the Reframing Faux Feelings chart (pages 88–89 in _Evoking Greatness_) to complete each sentence stem below based on the scenario provided.

Scenario: A new teacher complains that veteran teachers do not listen to him.

I'm guessing you might be feeling _____.

(Select a word from Column Two, *Possible Primary Feelings*)

Because your need for _____ *might be stirred up.*

(Select a word from Column Three, *Possible Underlying Needs*)

I wonder how that lands with you.

Scenario: A student is upset because there is never anyone to play with on the playground.

I'm guessing you might be feeling _____.

(Select a word from Column Two, *Possible Primary Feelings*)

That might make you _____.

(Select a word from Column Three, *Possible Underlying Needs*)

Have I got it right?

Scenario: A principal learns that the Superintendent has recommended to the school board that all continuation students be served on her campus.

I'm guessing you might be feeling _____.

(Select a word from Column Two, *Possible Primary Feelings*)

And that you might be needing _____.

(Select a word from Column Three, *Possible Underlying Needs*)

Have I understood or is it something else?

Scenario: A friend shares with you that she has decided her children are entirely selfish and never think of anyone but themselves.

That could make you _____.

(Select a word from Column Two, *Possible Primary Feelings*)

I guess your need for _____ *could be really strong right now.*

(Select a word from Column Three, *Possible Underlying Needs*)

Have I got it right?

Think about a few times you heard someone (that someone might have been you) use one of the words in the "Causal Attribution"

Don't be concerned if your statements seem awkward at this point. You are learning the essential ingredients for an empathetic statement. Smoothness of delivery will come with practice.

column of the "Reframing Causal Attributions" table in Chapter 4. Based on the situation you are recalling and what you have just practiced about expressing empathy, write an empathetic restatement of the judgment that you heard (or the one you made). For example, if you heard someone say, "There is too much to do already. I'm over-worked; there is no way I can take on anything else," a reframing might be: "I'm guessing you might be feeling resentful and tired, and that you might be needing more consideration and probably some rest. Have I understood?"

_____

_____

_____

_____

_____

_____

Activity 4.6 Reframing Causal Attributions

After recalling a real conversation in which you heard someone make a judgment, write down the causal attribution that was expressed. Then create an empathetic reframing of the primary feeling and underlying need. Again, the Reframing Causal Attributions chart (pages 97–98 in *Evocative Coaching*) or the Reframing Faux Feelings chart (pages 88–89 in *Evoking Greatness*) will be useful while completing this activity.

Often we react to expressions of frustration with sympathy or problem solving. This is an opportunity for authentic practice of a new way of responding.

Causal attribution heard: _____

Empathetic reframing:

_____

_____

_____

_____

_____

_____

_____

_____

Causal attribution heard: _____

Empathetic reframing:

_____

_____

_____

_____

_____

_____

_____

_____

_____

_____

Causal attribution heard: _____

Empathetic reframing:

_____

_____

_____

_____

_____

_____

_____

_____

_____

_____

_____

Listening Compassionately

The chart that follows can help us focus as we listen to our coachee recounting a story that has stirred up some strong feelings for them. We may hear them make evaluations as we hear another's story, but we want to avoid repeating them, reinforcing the thinking that has them stuck. This chart gives us a place to put those evaluations, but we would keep what's recorded under "The Story I'm Telling Myself" to ourselves. Our focus, instead, will be on discerning "The Heart of the Matter," the feelings and needs. It's here that there is space for new insights and growth.

Activity 4.7 Compassionate Listening Interview

Interview someone about a difficult experience. Complete the chart that follows as you listen.

What happened?	
The Story I'm Telling Myself (evaluations)	*The Heart of the Matter (feelings and needs)*

Connection Requests
For example:
• *Is there more you would like me to hear?*
• *Would you be willing to tell me what you're hearing me say?*
• *Would you be willing to tell me what comes up for you when you hear me say this?*

Action Requests
Would you be willing to ...?

Interlude

The Learning Brief

///

To make the transition from the no-fault turn to the strengths-building turn, it is helpful to draft a learning brief with the coachee. The purpose of the Learning Brief is to draft a plan for what the coachee will work on and how the coach will support them in their work. The Learning Brief contents should not be too general or too specific. In addition to clarifying goals, the Learning Brief also clarifies basic expectations regarding the approach taken by the coach and includes logistics as to how, where, when, and for how long the coaching conversations will take place. Having clarity about these elements is what distinguishes coaching from polite conversation or commiseration.

To practice using the Learning Brief, review the Learning Brief Template below and then draft your own Learning Brief to reflect on the work you would like to do to strengthen your skills as a coach.

Learning Brief Template

Coachee: _____Coach:_____Date:_____
Presenting Situation (What are the contexts and considerations for our work together? What does the coachee want to focus on?):
Underlying Needs & Values (What is really important to pay attention to, respect, and honor? What does the coachee value most?):
Desired Outcomes (What would improve or even transform this situation for the coachee? What does the coachee want to learn?):
Work Plan (What and how will we work together? Be specific as to the parameters of the coaching relationship.):

Activity: Consider your work with a particular coachee. Reflect on that coaching relationship as you develop a learning brief for your development as a coach.

Learning Brief

Coachee: _____Coach:_____Date:_____

Presenting Situation (What are the contexts and considerations for our work together? What does the coachee want to focus on?):

Underlying Needs & Values (What is really important to pay attention to, respect, and honor? What does the coachee value most?):

Desired Outcomes (What would improve or even transform this situation for the coachee? What does the coachee want to learn?):

Work Plan (What and how will we work together? Be specific as to the parameters of the coaching relationship.):

Practice for Appreciate Strengths

5

Appreciative Inquiry transforms our thinking from a deficit model of "What's wrong?" to a strengths-based model of "What's right?" We have been trained to solve problems by wearing our "fix it" hat. As a coach, we have "been there and done that" and we know how to solve the problem. However, we want our clients to focus on strengths rather than deficits so they can produce better and more lasting change and find joy in the process. Interviews with clients help coaches discover generative and life-giving forces—the positive core of coaching when it's at its best.

Activity 5.1 Appreciative Inquiry

Reflect on each of these four questions from the **Appreciative Inquiry "standard protocol"** and then write your responses in the box provided.

Best Experiences: Tell about your best teaching, coaching, or leadership experience—a time when you felt most alive and engaged. What made it so rewarding?

_____

_____

_____

_____

_____

_____

_____

_____

_____

_____

_____

_____

_____

_____

_____

_____

_____

_____

_____

_____

_____

Core Values: What do you value most deeply? Share about yourself, your relationships, and your professional work. Who are you when you are at your very best?

_____

_____

_____

_____

_____

_____

_____

_____

_____

_____

_____

_____

_____

_____

_____

_____

_____

_____

_____

_____

_____

_____

_____

_____

_____

_____

_____

_____

_____

_____

_____

_____

Supporting Conditions: What are the key ingredients, both internal and external, that enable you to be at your best and to truly enjoy what you do?

_____

_____

_____

_____

_____

_____

_____

_____

_____

_____

_____

_____

_____

_____

_____

_____

_____

_____

_____

_____

_____

_____

_____

_____

_____

_____

_____

_____

_____

_____

Three Wishes: Tell about your hopes and dreams for your coaching practice. If you could make any three wishes for your coaching practice come true, what would they be?

_____

_____

_____

_____

_____

_____

_____

_____

_____

_____

_____

_____

_____

_____

_____

_____

_____

_____

_____

_____

_____

_____

_____

_____

_____

_____

_____

_____

_____

_____

Appreciative Inquiry is undergirded by five principles: the positive, constructionist, simultaneity, anticipatory, and poetic principles. These principles are related to each other and work together to generate positive actions and outcomes.

Activity 5.2 Appreciative Inquiry Principles

Write a brief description of each of the five principles of Appreciative Inquiry (pages 108–111 in *Evocative Coaching* or pages 101–103 in *Evoking Greatness*).

Positivity Principle:

_____

_____

_____

_____

_____

_____

_____

_____

_____

_____

_____

_____

Constructionist Principle:

_____

_____

_____

_____

_____

_____

_____

_____

_____

_____

_____

_____

_____

_____

_____

Simultaneity Principle:

_____
_____
_____
_____
_____
_____
_____
_____
_____
_____

Anticipatory Principle:

_____
_____
_____
_____
_____
_____
_____
_____
_____
_____

Poetic Principle:

_____
_____
_____
_____
_____
_____
_____
_____
_____
_____

SOAR

SOAR illuminates the best of what it is and what it might be. It is easy for positive realities to get lost in the continuous clamor of day-to-day deadlines and difficulties. Positive, strengths-based data can reframe a situation and set things on a positive course. It is the work of evocative coaching to look for those strengths and to arm leaders with an understanding of what they are doing well. To do this, evocative coaches put the five principles of Appreciative Inquiry into action by engaging in a SOAR analysis with clients, inquiring into the coachee's Strengths (S), Opportunities (O), Aspirations (A), and Resources (R) to discover the best of what is and to imagine the best of what might be. SOAR fosters new realities and evokes a way to help our coachees believe in their ability to make a significant impact.

Activity 5.3 SOAR

Reflect on yourself as an evocative coach, and your desire is to evoke the greatness in those you are coaching. Respond to the prompts below.

How do you or how do you hope to, as a coach, pay attention to what is positive—to your strengths—and what has worked well for you in the past?

Strengths:

_____

_____

_____

_____

_____

_____

_____

_____

_____

_____

Opportunities:

_____

_____

_____

_____

_____

_____

_____

_____

_____

_____

Opportunities are expressions of what you would like to learn, explore, and do as a coach. What would you like to pay more attention to in your coaching?

Aspirations:

_____

_____

_____

_____

_____

_____

_____

_____

_____

_____

_____

_____

_____

_____

_____

_____

Aspirations capture who we are and who we want to be as a coach. They are expressions of identity and mastery. Imagine who you are when you are at your very best as a coach. What do you aspire to be as a coach that makes a significant impact?

///////////////////////////////

To be effective, teachers and leaders must pay attention to the resources that are either available or can be marshaled to bring their aspirations for themselves and their classes, schools, or districts into being. What resources for you, as a coach, most readily come to mind to bring your aspirations to fruition?

Resources:

_____

_____

_____

_____

_____

_____

_____

_____

_____

_____

_____

_____

_____

_____

_____

_____

_____

_____

_____

_____

_____

_____

_____

_____

_____

_____

_____

_____

_____

Practice for Design for Action

6

Coaching is not complete unless it moves to actionable steps—to an experiment. We don't only want wonderful, empathetic, feel-good conversations. We want wonderful, empathetic, feel-good conversations that inspire and generate behavior change. Without behavior change, coaching has fallen short of the mark. Evocative coaching uses design thinking to inspire confidence, to invite possibilities, and to implement new ideas. The heart of the design thinking process is to map out experiments that will assist educational leaders to learn more about themselves and how they can be successful in life and work. Design thinking is based on positive relationship, positive images, positive energy and emotions, and positive actions.

A Design Experiment includes a hypothesis, procedures, materials, data recording, commitment, observations, and conclusions.

Sample Hypothesis: **IF**…I consciously strive to ask my coachee about their strengths and vitalities, with the help of appreciative interviews, assessments, and observations, **THEN**…they will be more prone to invite opportunities and frame aspirations.

Activity 6.1 Hypothesis

Write an "If…then…" statement that describes an aspiration you have for yourself as an evocative coach whose mission is to inspire the greatness in your coachee.

Example: **If** I consciously strive to ask my coachee about their strengths and vitalities, with the help of appreciative interviews, assessments, and observations, **then** they will be more likely to invite opportunities and frame aspirations for those with whom they work.

If

_____

_____

_____

_____

_____

_____

Then

_____

_____

_____

_____

_____

A strong hypothesis will move you to action. It should be about something that you are motivated to do, not what you think you should do.

Relevance: Next, articulate how your hypothesis is relevant to an important goal or professional standard.

Sample Relevance Statement: *I want to be a coach that takes off my "fix it" hat and connects my coachees to their sense of self-efficacy so they can achieve their aspirations and be successful and confident.*

Activity 6.2 Relevance

Write a statement that connects your hypothesis to an important goal.

_____

_____

_____

_____

_____

_____

_____

Often a reference to a professional standard demonstrates "relevance" of a hypothesis. But it may also be relevant because of a personal goal.

_____

_____

_____

_____

_____

_____

After developing a hypothesis and explaining its relevance, the next step in the design process is to identify the strategies or activities that will be used to test the hypothesis. It's also necessary to determine the systems and resources that will be needed as well as determine when the activities will be completed.

Example:

STRATEGIES OR ACTIVITIES (SPECIFIC AS TO WHY, WHERE, AND HOW)	SYSTEMS AND RESOURCES NEEDED	TIMELINE
Make a list of Appreciative Inquiry questions I will ask my coachees	LEAD Folder _Evoking Greatness_ book Appreciative Inquiry protocol questions	Have the list complete one week before our next conversation

Activity 6.3 Strategies

List the strategies you will use, the resources you'll need, and the timeline needed to test your hypothesis about inspiring greatness in your coachee.

It's essential to collect data and determine how it will be reported. Otherwise we won't know whether or not our hypothesis is true or false.

Strategies	Resources Needed	Timeline

It's useful to first brainstorm possible strategies and then list the ones you decide will lead to your goal and are practical.

Activity 6.4 Data Collection

Identify tangible ways you will verify to yourself that you have increased your knowledge, skills, and actions as an evocative coach (based on your stated hypothesis).

Describe Data Collection and Reporting Techniques:

_____

_____

_____

_____

_____

_____

_____

_____

_____

Often the most effective sources of data are the documents you are going to produce as part of the process. Data can be calendars, agendas, minutes, journal entries, as well as records of results.

We have found that having a coachee identify on a scale from 1 to 10 their confidence that they will complete the activities and collect the data provides incredible insights.

Activity 6.5 Confidence Level

On a scale of 1–10 what is your confidence that you will complete the activities and collect the data that you have written above?

Confidence Level (On a Scale of 1–10): _____
    Revise the strategy, systems, resources, timeline, and/or data collections until your confidence level is "7" or higher.

Asking a coachee to describe why they picked the number they did reveals important information.

Making use of the design template enables coaches and their coachees to develop an experiment that meets the requirements of a traditional SMART goal (specific, measurable, attainable, relevant, and time bound). But, because we have created an experiment, we also evaluate and refine. In doing so, we create a SMARTER goal.

A design template assists us to move successfully from ideas to action by adding procedural clarity to the design of the experiments, thus reducing performance anxiety. The blank Design Template in the Resources section may be used to assist coaches in this process.

Activity 6.6 A Complete Coaching Conversation

You now understand the four steps of evocative coaching: Listen, Empathize, Appreciate, and Design. Use the prompts in the four pages of the LEAD folder in the Resources section to guide you as you complete the evocative coaching "dance" with a partner. The topic you choose is wide open. Find it through mindful, calm, attentive, reflective, and imaginative listening.

Use the experimental design template on the following page to record how your coachee will achieve the aspiration discovered during the conversation.

EXPERIMENTAL DESIGN

Name:_____**Date:** _____

Focus (Check): *Professional_____Personal_____*

State Hypothesis:

Describe Relevance to Personal Aspirations / Professional Standards:

Strategies or Activities (Specific as to What, Where, & How):	**Supporting Systems & Resources:**	**Timeline:**

Describe Data Collection & Reporting Techniques:

Confidence Level (On a Scale of 0 to 10): _____

Revise the strategy, systems, resources, and / or timeline until confidence is 7 or higher.

Practice for the Dynamic Flow of Change

7

One way to understand our goal in discussing environments with our coachees is that we want to assist them to get into "flow" while conducting their SMART experiments. The notion of "flow" is a concept identified, studied, and developed by psychologist, Mihaly Csikszentmihalyi (Csikszentmihalyi, 1990). Athletes sometimes describe it as "being in the zone." Csikszentmihalyi has studied high-performing people in various endeavors including athletes, musicians, rock climbers, and chess players. They all report moments when time seems to disappear and performance peaks.

After years of research, Csikszentmihalyi came to define flow as "the experience of being fully immersed in and unusually successful with an activity" (Tschannen-Moran & Tschannen-Moran, 2018, p. 142). For that to happen, he determined that activities must balance the challenge of the task with the skill of the person. They also must be intrinsically motivated and provide opportunities for specific, immediate, real-time feedback. It's hard to experience flow when challenges are assigned against our will, when we don't know how we are doing, or when they are scaled inappropriately. That's why tasks that are too hard generate anxiety and tasks that are too easy generate boredom.

As coaches in schools, we pay attention to these dynamics with our coachees. How they are feeling about the prospects of their experiments will influence and may determine their success. When they are feeling anxious or bored, that is a sign that we may want to adjust the challenge or skill level appropriately. We also want to explore their motivation and feedback loops. People get into flow when they conduct challenging SMARTER experiments that are just within reach. Those are the experiments that get people focused on leaning into the learning.

Activity 7.1 Flow

Recall personal experiences with *Flow*. Write about an experience you had with *Flow*.

Think of a time when you were so engaged in a higher-level cognitive task in which you lost all sense of time.

_____

_____

_____

_____

_____

_____

_____

_____

_____

_____

_____

_____

_____

_____

_____

_____

_____

_____

_____

Evocative coaches always talk with our coachees about their environments. If we fail to have that conversation, then we may be missing important elements of the coaching equation. Performance is not just a matter of motivation and skills. That's why "Supporting Systems & Resources" is on the Experimental Design Template. The following questions help us focus on environmental concerns:

- How could environments be modified so as to make you more effective, to better enhance your ongoing professional development, and to infuse you with more energy, enjoyment, and fulfillment at work?

- What would you like more of?

- What would you like less of?

- What would help you to be more successful and fulfilled?

Activity 7.2 Environmental Factors

Find a partner with whom you can practice having a coaching conversation in which you design an experiment about the environmental factors that would better support their work. Use the Experimental Design Template to summarize that conversation.

One way to increase self-efficacy is to uncover and explore the conflicting feelings and needs that may be holding people back from change. Instead of pushing people to get over their ambivalence, we can roll with their resistance until it comes unglued. Resistance is not usually caused by malevolence. It is rather a common and normal part of life as we sort through our competing commitments.

The Immunity to Change process developed by Harvard psychologists Robert Kegan and Lisa Lahey (2009) is a useful process for coming to terms with this resistance. In this process, we guide our coachee to examine competing commitments (what is holding us back), to explore big assumptions (underlying fears and catastrophizing), and to field test new possibilities (baby steps).

Activity 7.3 Immunity to Change

After reviewing the *Immunity to Change* process (pages 177–181 in *Evocative Coaching* or pages 148–152 in *Evoking Greatness*) use the Immunity Map that follows to guide a discussion with a volunteer.

EXPERIMENTAL DESIGN

Name:_____Date: _____

Focus (Check): *Professional_____Personal_____*

State Hypothesis:

Describe Relevance to Personal Aspirations / Professional Standards:

Strategies or Activities (Specific as to What, Where, & How):	**Supporting Systems & Resources:**	**Timeline:**

Describe Data Collection & Reporting Techniques:

Confidence Level (On a Scale of 0 to 10): _____

Revise the strategy, systems, resources, and / or timeline until confidence is 7 or higher.

Develop a plan to confront something they have been procrastinating or putting off, or perhaps where, for some reason, there has been a lack of follow-through.

A sense of urgency can be very strong when we see or hear something we don't like or when we have an idea that we want to share as to how someone could do something better. Evocative coaches take the time to gain clear understandings of what is going on, of what the person we are coaching needs, of what they want to learn, and of how we are going to work together. Unfortunately, most people have had experience with mentoring or supervising that did not take learning preferences into consideration. It's easy for a coach to fall into traps that interfere with the work of evoking the greatness that lies within those we are coaching. Review the common traps for coaches (pages 185–188 in *Evocative Coaching* or pages 154–156 in *Evoking Greatness*).

Activity 7.4 Coaching Traps

In your own words, define the traps listed below and write one or two strategies a coach can utilize to avoid falling into each particular trap.

Fix-it Trap

Definition:

_____

_____

_____

_____

Strategies to avoid this trap:

_____

_____

_____

_____

_____

_____

_____

Immunity Map Worksheet

Name:_____Date:_____

Commitment (Improvement goals)	Doing / Not Doing Instead (Behaviors that work against the goals)	Hidden Competing Commitments	Big Assumptions
		Worry Box:	

Adapted from Kegan, R., & Lahey, L. L. (2009). *Immunity to Change: How to overcome it and unlock the potential in yourself and your organization*. Boston, MA: Harvard Business School Press.

Cheerleader Trap

Definition:

_____

_____

_____

_____

Strategies to avoid this trap:

_____

_____

_____

_____

_____

_____

_____

Rabbit-hole Trap

Definition:

_____

_____

_____

_____

Strategies to avoid this trap:

_____

_____

_____

_____

_____

Hurry-hurry Trap

Definition:

_____

_____

_____

_____

Strategies to avoid this trap:

Yes-but Trap

Definition:

Strategies to avoid this trap:

One Right Way Trap

Definition:

Strategies to avoid this trap:

Practice for the Reflective Coach

8

Evocative coaching invites coaches to launch into a journey of "trial and correction," always seeking effective ways to guide the learning and growth of the teachers, school, and district leaders we coach. Evocative coaches *reflect-in-action* by thinking on our feet, being aware of our feelings and being mindfully present during coaching conversations to respond appropriately. Evocative coaches *reflect-on-action* by planning what we hope to accomplish and reviewing what actually took place in our conversations. By recording our coaching sessions and reflecting and analyzing using tools found in the book that quantify our actions such as charting talk time, coaching behaviors, and noticing style points, coaches design experiments to strengthen evocative coaching skills.

Activity 8.1 Reflecting on Action

Record a coaching session. Select observation tools from the resources in the text or this book to analyze your coaching.

Tools available for reflection "on action" (from Resources section):

- Coaching Observation Tool

- Style Points

- Charting Talk Time

- Charting Coaching Behaviors

///////////////////////////////
*What are your
strengths?*

///////////////////////////////
*What went
well?*

///////////////////////////////
*What surprised
you when
using the tools
to reflect on
your session?*

_____

At the end of every coaching session, we have an opportunity to enhance our learning and inform and improve our practice as coaches by asking for appreciative feedback. We can ask for example:

- What did you value most about this coaching session?

- What would you like me to do differently next time?

- How could I better assist you to reach your goals?

Activity 8.2 Feedback

After your next coaching session, remember to ask your coachee for appreciative feedback. Ask about what you did or said during the session that was particularly helpful to them. And/or ask for feedback using the *Session Feedback Form* that you will find in the Resources section.

_____

_____

_____

_____

_____

_____

_____

_____

_____

_____

_____

_____

_____

_____

_____

_____

_____

_____

_____

_____

_____

_____

_____

_____

_____

Talk with a trusted partner about what you discovered by asking for feedback.

Record what you learned here.

Coaches bring their talents and strengths to each conversation. Pay attention to how our strengths support us to become the coaches we aspire to become. One tool for discovering strengths, based on the classification of strengths developed by Person and Seligman, is the Values-in-Action (VIA) Signature Strengths questionnaire. The questionnaire can be taken online, free of charge.

Activity 8.3 VIA Strengths Survey

Take the **VIA Signature Strengths** questionnaire at www.authentichappiness.sas.upenn.edu. You will need to register to establish an account; however, there is no cost or obligation to take the survey. Once on the web page, you will find the survey in the *Questionnaire* section. Click on the arrow and scroll down.

////////////////////////////

Share your most used strengths with a friend. What was surprising?

_____

_____

_____

_____

_____

_____

_____

_____

_____

_____

_____

_____

_____

_____

_____

_____

_____

_____

_____

_____

_____

_____

_____

Activity 8.4 Cultivating Strengths

Review your strengths and determine a strength you are not using as often but would like to cultivate. Talk with a coaching partner or close associate to brainstorm ways to have that quality show up more frequently during coaching. Then take this a step further and use experimental design to create a plan to actually cultivate a less-used strength.

_____

_____

_____

_____

_____

_____

_____

_____

_____

_____

_____

_____

_____

_____

_____

_____

_____

_____

_____

_____

_____

_____

_____

_____

_____

_____

_____

_____

Don't stop before you have at least ten ideas.

EXPERIMENTAL DESIGN

Name:_____Date: _____

Focus (Check): *Professional_____Personal_____*

State Hypothesis:

Describe Relevance to Personal Aspirations / Professional Standards:

Strategies or Activities (Specific as to What, Where, & How):	Supporting Systems & Resources:	Timeline:

Describe Data Collection & Reporting Techniques:

Confidence Level (On a Scale of 0 to 10): _____

Revise the strategy, systems, resources, and / or timeline until confidence is 7 or higher.

Activity 8.5 Your New Coaching Platform

At the end of Chapter 1, you were asked to develop a coaching platform. It was our hope that writing a platform would clarify your focus as you completed the activities in this book. Now that you have concluded the activities, please write a new coaching platform. A comparison of the two versions will provide you with insight into how you have grown as a coach as a result of your reflection and practice.

What are the basic values, beliefs, and ethical standards that will inform your coaching practice? How do you hope to enhance the professional development of those with whom you work?

What will you do to become the coach you just described?

_____

_____

_____

_____

_____

_____

_____

_____

_____

_____

_____

_____

_____

_____

_____

_____

_____

_____

_____

_____

_____

_____

_____

_____

_____

_____

You may recall that a coaching platform states clearly and concisely how you understand the purpose of coaching as well as how you frame your aspirations and view your possibilities for fulfilling that purpose. Our coaching platforms are dynamic wishes for how we intended to show up for our coachees. They evolve over time as we do and can be reimagined often. Over the years of your practice as an evocative coach, please repeat this activity; doing so will focus and celebrate your work.

Conclusion

The four steps of evocative coaching (Story, Empathy, Inquiry, and Design) can be learned in a minute; however, mastering them is a lifetime opportunity.

The use of audio and video recordings of your coaching sessions, followed by your own reflections in action and reflections on action, will provide powerful insight to you. We encourage you to print multiple copies of the Coaching Style Sheet to use in such reflection. Doing so is a powerful tool to advance your coaching journey. We also encourage you to make use of the resources in the Resources section of this book for lists of coaching questions and reminders about the principles that undergird evocative coaching.

Additionally, we urge you to create or join a community of coaches as you move beyond this Practice Guide to transform the work of those you coach. Thank you for making these activities a part of your journey.

The No-Fault Turn

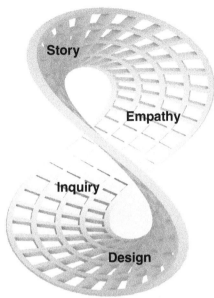

The Strengths-Building Turn

The Möbius Model of Evocative Coaching.

Resources

///

Many evocative coaches have found the following tools to be useful in their coaching. Some have been created by coaches as they strive to incorporate the principles of evocative coaching into their practice. Others are examples of the types of information coaches can gather (at the request of their coachees) to be shared without evaluation or judgment.

Please feel free to use these tools in their current form or to adapt them to your specific needs. It is our hope that the resources you develop may find themselves added to a future edition of this practice guide.

Coaching Session Feedback Form

Coach's Name:_____Your Name:_____Date:_____

As one of many ways to encourage coaching proficiency, please give your coach feedback using this form after a coaching session. On a five-point scale, to what extent do you agree or disagree with the following statements?

1 = Totally Disagree, 2 = Somewhat Disagree, 3 = Partly Agree, 4 = Mostly Agree, 5 = Totally Agree

Proficiencies					
Story Listening	1	2	3	4	5
1. My coach listened carefully and fully to me.					
2. My coach explored what I had to say and opened up new understandings.					
Expressing Empathy	1	2	3	4	5
3. I felt accepted and respected by my coach.					
4. My coach helped me to understand the things I need and value most.					
Appreciative Inquiry	1	2	3	4	5
5. My coach asked powerful, strengths-based questions.					
6. My coach explored the upside of observational data (what is going on).					
7. I developed a larger sense of my aspirations and potential through this conversation.					
Design Thinking	1	2	3	4	5
8. My coach brainstormed ideas and possibilities with me.					
9. Something new came out of this conversation that I am confident I will follow through on.					
10. We talked about ways to make the environment in which I work more supportive.					
Coaching Presence	1	2	3	4	5
11. My coach worked with me as a curious collaborator rather than as an expert advisor.					
12. I did not feel pushed to do what my coach wanted me to do.					
13. I really enjoyed, appreciated, and valued this conversation.					

14. What was the best part of this coaching session?

15. What was your biggest take-away from this coaching session?

16. How has your thinking or plans changed as a result of this coaching session?

17. How could your coach be even more helpful to you in the future?

Evocative Coaching (Listen-Empathy-Ask-Design) "LEAD" Strategies for Strengths-Based School Transformation (for Teachers)

L	**Listen to their Story.....** • *mindfully* • *calmly* • *openly* • *attentively* • *quietly* • *reflectively* • *imaginatively*	Tell me the story of how you came to be a teacher. Tell me a story that illustrates what has been working well for you. Tell me a story about a time when you handled a tough situation well. Tell me a story about a time when you felt you made a real contribution. Tell me a story that illustrates what you love most about your work. Tell me a story about a time when you had a lot of fun in the classroom. Tell me a story that illustrates how your values come through in your teaching. Tell me a story about a time when you felt connected to one of your students. Tell me a story about a time when you tried something new. Tell me a story about a time when your lesson plan went surprisingly well.	
E	**Empathize...** • *Make observations (not evaluations)* • *Clarify feelings* • *Understand needs* • *Make requests (not demands)*	**Feelings When Needs Are Not Being Met:** **Hostile** (animosity, appalled, disdain, cold, scorn, vengeful) **Angry** (enraged, furious, irate, livid, incensed, mad, outraged) **Annoyed** (aggravated, impatient, cross, grouchy, irritated, bitter) **Upset** (agitated, alarmed, restless, disturbed, rattled, unsettled) **Tense** (antsy, anxious, distressed, stressed, overwhelmed, nervous) **Afraid** (apprehensive, dread, fear, hesitant, mistrustful, wary, timid)	**Feelings When Needs Are Being Met:** **Exhilarated** (ecstatic, elated, enthralled, exuberant, giddy) **Excited** (alive, amazed, animated, eager, energetic, enthusiastic) **Inspired** (amazed, astonished, awed, dazzled, thrilled, radiant) **Joyful** (amused, delighted, elated, ecstatic, pleased, gleeful, happy) **Relaxed** (at ease, carefree, open, comfortable) **Curious** (adventurous, alert interested, intrigued, fascinated)
A	**Ask Appreciative Questions (Inquiry)....** • *Discover strengths* • *Observe vitalities* • *Frame aspirations* • *Invite possibilities*	What would you like to pay more attention to in your classroom? What possibilities do you see for yourself in the next few months? What changes do you think your students would really appreciate? What variables do you think matter most? What would you like to see more of in your classroom? How could your needs and the needs of your students be more fully met? What kind of environment would you like to create for your students? What things are most important to you right now in life? In work? What changes would excite you and make you feel great? How would you describe your intentions over the next few months? What would your life be like if you realized those intentions? What are the best things that could happen in your classroom in the near future? What do you think are the best possible outcomes of our work together?	
D	**Design Next Steps....** • *Brainstorm ideas* • *Frame designs as experiments* • *Increase confidence* • *Secure commitment*	**BEFORE EXPERIMENT:** What ideas stand out as the best? Which ones would be the most fun? The most rewarding? What would it take to succeed with this idea? What strengths might you leverage? What kind of impact might they have? Which ones do you want to try first? How would you rate your confidence? What will you do?	**AFTER EXPERIMENT:** What parts of the experiment can we celebrate? What skills were you using well? What approaches worked for students? What hopes did you have for the lesson? What might have happened if you had chosen to do something different? How can you build on this experience for even better results next time?

Evocative Coaching (Story-Empathy-Inquiry-Design) "LEAD" Strategies for Strengths-Based School Transformation (for Leaders)

L	**Listen to their Story.....** • *mindfully* • *calmly* • *openly* • *attentively* • *quietly* • *reflectively* • *imaginatively*	• Tell me the story of how you came to be a leader. • Tell me a story that illustrates what has been working well for you. • Tell me a story about a time when you handled a tough situation well. • Tell me a story about a time when you felt you made a real contribution. • Tell me a story that illustrates what you love most about your work. • Tell me a story about a time when you had a lot of fun in the faculty meeting. • Tell me a story that illustrates how your values come through in your leadership. • Tell me a story about a time when you felt connected to one of your teachers. • Tell me a story about a time when you tried something new. • Tell me a story about a time when an evaluation conference with a teacher went surprisingly well.		
E	**Empathize...** • *Make observations (not evaluations)* • *Clarify feelings* • *Understand needs* • *Make requests (not demands)*	**Feelings When Needs Are Not Being Met:** **Hostile** (animosity, appalled, disdain, cold, scorn, vengeful) **Angry** (enraged, furious, irate, livid, incensed, mad, outraged) **Annoyed** (aggravated, impatient, cross, grouchy, irritated, bitter) **Upset** (agitated, alarmed, restless, disturbed, rattled, unsettled) **Tense** (antsy, anxious, distressed, stressed, overwhelmed, nervous) **Afraid** (apprehensive, dread, fear, hesitant, mistrustful, wary, timid)	**Feelings When Needs Are Being Met:** **Exhilarated** (ecstatic, elated, enthralled, exuberant, giddy) **Excited** (alive, amazed, animated, eager, energetic, enthusiastic) **Inspired** (amazed, astonished, awed, dazzled, thrilled, radiant) **Joyful** (amused, delighted, elated, ecstatic, pleased, gleeful, happy) **Relaxed** (at ease, carefree, open, comfortable) **Curious** (adventurous, alert, interested, intrigued, fascinated)	
A	**Ask Appreciative Questions (Inquiry)....** • *Discover strengths* • *Observe vitalities* • *Frame aspirations* • *Invite possibilities*	• What would you like to pay more attention to in your school? • What possibilities do you see for yourself in the next few months? • What changes do you think your teachers would really appreciate? • What variables do you think matter most? • What would you like to see more of in your school? • How could your needs and the needs of your teachers be more fully met? • What kind of environment would you like to create for your school? • What things are most important to you right now in life? In work? • What changes would excite you and make you feel great? • How would you describe your intentions over the next few months? • What would your life be like if you realized those intentions? • What are the best things that could happen in your school in the near future? • What do you think are the best possible outcomes of our work together?		
D	**Design Next Steps....** • *Brainstorm ideas* • *Frame designs as experiments* • *Increase confidence* • *Secure commitment*	**BEFORE EXPERIMENT:** • What ideas stand out as the best? • Which ones would be the most fun? The most rewarding? • What would it take to succeed with this idea? • What strengths might you leverage? • What kind of impact might they have? • Which ones do you want to try first? • How would you rate your confidence? • What will you do?	**AFTER EXPERIMENT:** • What parts of the experiment can we celebrate? • What skills were you using well? • What approaches worked for teachers? • What hopes did you have for the school? • What might have happened if you had chosen to do something different? • How can you build on this experience for even better results next time?	

Stems for Evocative Coaching LEAD (Listen, Empathize, Ask Appreciative Questions, Design Next Steps)

| L | Listen to their Story...
 • *mindfully*
 • *calmly*
 • *openly*
 • *attentively*
 • *quietly*
 • *reflectively*
 • *imaginatively* | • Tell me the story of how you came to be a teacher/leader.
 • Tell me a story about how you came to lead/teach at this particular school.
 • Tell me a story that illustrates what has been working well for you.
 • Tell me a story about a time when you handled a tough situation well.
 • Tell me a story about a time when you felt you made a real contribution.
 • Tell me a story that illustrates what you love most about your work.
 • Tell me a story about a time when you had a lot of fun in your work.
 • Tell me a story that illustrates how your values come through in your teaching / in your leadership.
 • Tell me a story about an experience as a teacher / leader that taught you a valuable lesson.
 • Tell me a story about a time when you felt respected and honored as a teacher / school leader.
 • Tell me a story about a time when you felt connected to one of your teachers.
 • Tell me a story of a time when a change initiative went surprisingly well.
 • Tell me a story about a time when this school celebrated an outstanding achievement. What was that and when did it happen?
 • Tell me a story about an important decision that this school community faced and how it was made.
 • Tell me a story about a time when the school faced a significant challenge and was successful in meeting that challenge.
 • Tell me a story of a new teacher or staff member who joined the school community and became a real leader.
 • Tell me a story of a time when there was a conflict that divided the staff or the community. What were the competing interests and how was it resolved?
 • Tell me a story of someone who is considered a hero or heroine in this school. What are the traits that this school community valued in them.
 • Tell me a story of something really humorous that happened here.
 • Tell me a story of a time when people were playful or shared a good laugh together. |

Stems for Evocative Coaching LEAD, Continued

E	Empathize...	Causal Attribution	Primary Feelings	Underlying Needs
	• *Make observations (not evaluations)* • *Clarify feelings* • *Understand needs* • *Make requests (not demands)*	**Attacked** **Belittled** **Blamed** **Betrayed** **Boxed In** **Coerced** **Criticized** **Disrespected** **Distrusted** **Harassed** **Hassled** **Insulted** **Interrupted** **Manipulated** **Overworked** **Pressured** **Rejected** **Taken Advantage of** **Taken for Granted** **Tricked** **Unappreciated** **Unsupported** **Violated**	Angry, scared Outraged, embarrassed, tense Indignant, angry, scared, hurt Outraged, stunned, hurt Angry, frustrated, scared, anxious Angry, frustrated, anxious Irritated, scared, embarrassed Indignant, frustrated, hurt Frustrated, sad, hurt Angry, pressured, frightened Irritated, irked, frustrated Angry, incensed, embarrassed Resentful, irritated, hurt Angry, resentful, sad Resentful, angry, tired Resentful, overwhelmed, anxious Angry, defiant, scared, hurt Angry, frustrated, powerless Angry, disappointed, hurt Furious, indignant, embarrassed Frustrated, irritated, sad, hurt Resentful, sad, hurt Outraged, agitated, sad	Safety, respect Respect, appreciation Fairness, justice Trust, honesty, respect Autonomy, freedom, choice Autonomy, choice, efficacy Respect, understanding Respect, acknowledgment Honesty, integrity, trust Respect, consideration, ease Autonomy, ease, space, calm Respect, consideration Respect, consideration Autonomy, choice, power Respect, consideration, rest Relaxation, ease, space Belonging, acknowledgment Autonomy, choice Appreciation, respect Integrity, honesty, trust Appreciation, respect Support, understanding Safety, trust, space, respect
	Stems		I'm guessing you might be feeling ... I'm wondering if you are feeling ... That might make you ... And that could make you feel ...	Because you need (or value)_____ I'd guess your need for _____ could be really strong right now.

Stems for Evocative Coaching LEAD, Continued

| A | Ask Appreciative Questions (Inquiry)...

• *discover strengths*
• *observe vitalities*
• *frame aspirations*
• *invite possibilities* | • Tell me about your best experience of leading a group of people to a positive outcome, a time when your contribution and way of being helped the group accomplish something significant.
• Tell me about the things that matter most to you, that you value most deeply about yourself, your work, and your relationships. How are these core values expressed in your life and work?
• Recall a time when you worked in an environment where you were really at your best. What were the particular aspects of that context that brought out the best in you? How did you grow and what leadership qualities emerged under those conditions?
• Tell me about your hopes and dreams for the future. If you had three wishes that would make this school/district a more vibrant and positive learning environment, what would they be?
• What opportunities do you see for yourself and your school/district in the coming year?
• What would you like to pay more attention to in your school?
• What are the best things that could happen in your school in the near future?
• What results do you think are the most important?
• What new direction/initiatives excite you right now?
• What initiatives are working well and need to be strengthened and built upon?
• What excites you when you walk through classrooms?
• What would you like your leadership to look like a few months from now?
• What new skills would you like to cultivate moving forward? What opportunities are there to gain those skills?
• What things are most important to you right now? In work? In life?
• What changes do you think teachers would really appreciate? Parents? Students?
• What has worked for you in other settings that you can draw on in this situation?
• How would you describe your intentions over the next few months?
• What is something you would like to work on in the immediate future?
• What things can you imagine doing differently?
• What changes would excite and inspire you?
• What is something really important to pay attention to right now?
• What do you think are the best possible outcomes for our work together? |

Stems for Evocative Coaching LEAD, Continued

D	Design Next Steps...	BEFORE EXPERIMENT:	AFTER EXPERIMENT:
	• Brainstorm ideas • Frame designs as experiments • Increase confidence • Secure commitment	• What ideas stand out as the best? • Which ones would be the most fun? The most rewarding? • Which ideas would push you the most? • Which ideas might have the greatest impact? • What kind of impact might they have? • What would it take to succeed? • Which ideas build on what you are already doing well? • Which ideas would require you to learn new skills? • What makes them worth pursuing? • What attracts you to them? • How does this idea compare to other approaches? • How easy would they be to implement? • What strengths might you leverage? • When have you tried something like this before? • Which ones do you want to try first? • What data will you use to measure your progress and success?	• What parts of the experiment can we celebrate? • What skills were you using well? • What approaches worked for teachers? For students? For parents? • What hopes did you have? • What strengths did you call upon to make this experiment a success? • What might have happened if you had chosen to do something different? • How did you grow and what did you learn? • What surprised you? • What do you hope to build on going forward? • How did you feel before, during and after the experiment? • At this point, what did the data collected tell us? (Evaluate) • What additional resources were needed? (Refine) • How can you build on this experience for even better results next time? (Innovate) • What are the logical "next steps"?

Experimental Design

EXPERIMENTAL DESIGN
Name:_____Date: _____ **Focus (Check):** *Professional_____Personal_____*
State Hypothesis:
Describe Relevance to Personal Aspirations / Professional Standards:

Strategies or Activities (Specific as to What, Where, & How):	Supporting Systems & Resources:	Timeline:

Describe Data Collection & Reporting Techniques:

Confidence Level (On a Scale of 0 to 10): _____ *Revise the strategy, systems, resources, and / or timeline until confidence is 7 or higher.*

Coaching Observation Tool

Coach:_____   Observer:_____   Date:_____

EC COACHING STRATEGIES	COACHING MOVES AND COACHING LANGUAGE
L Listen to their story • *Establish rapport* • *Celebrate progress* • *Explore stories* • *Listen attentively*	
E Empathize • *Express empathy* • *Clarify focus*	
A Ask Appreciative Questions • *Discover strengths* • *Explore opportunities* • *Frame aspirations* • *Identify resources*	
D Design Next Steps • *Brainstorm ideas* • *Design a SMARTER experiment* • *Confirm commitment* • *Roll with resistance* • *Explore culture change* • *Seek feedback*	

Using Evocative Coaching Style Points
(No Fault Turn with Prompts)

Attentive listening—mindful, calm, open, reflective	**Story Listening**
	
	• Establish Rapport
	
	• Celebrate Progress
	
	• Exploring Stories: vantage, pivot, lesson points
		What word or words captures your energy at this point in time?
		
		Tell me a little about yourself.
		
		Why did you choose to make teaching your career?
		
		Tell me a story that illustrates what you love most about your work.
		    Tell it again with a change in…
		    Tell it again AS IF this really happened.

Attentive listening—mindful, calm, open, reflective	**Expressing Empathy** • Empathy Reflections: observations, feelings, needs, requests • Clarifying Focus	After identifying feelings and needs ask: Did I get that right? or Would you be willing to tell me what you heard me say?" or How do you feel when you hear me say that?"

Using Evocative Coaching Style Points
(Strengths-Building Turn with Prompts)

Attentive listening—mindful, calm, open, refelctive, imaginative	**Appreciative Inquiry** • Discovering Strengths • Exploring Opportunities • Framing Aspirations • Identifying Resources	What are you most proud of so far? With this in mind, what would you wish for this year? What is already working for you? What has worked in other situations that might work here? What would success look like? Feel like? How would this reflect what is important to you? How close are you to that success? (0= not on the radar, 10= it's always with me) What would you like more of? How would you like your situation to be different a few moths from now?	

Attentive Listening—mindful, calm, open, refelctive, imaginative	**Design Thinking**
	• Brainstorming Ideas
	
	• Designing a SMARTER Experiment
	
	• Confirming Commitment
	
	• Rolling with Resistance
	
	• Exploring Culture Change
		How about brainstorming with me ... 5—6 out-of-box ideas
		
		Which of these ideas
		    is most intriguing to work on right away?
		    could you begin working with right away?
		How might you get started? When?
		
		Is there someone who can help you?
		What do you need? How can you get it?
		
		On a scale of 0—10, how sure are you that you will actually try out this idea?
		
		Would you have thought of this if we hadn't talked?	

	• Session Feedback		

Using Evocative Coaching Style Points
(No-Fault Turn)

Attentive listening—mindful, calm, open, reflective	**Story Listening** • Establish Rapport • Appreciative Questions • Exploring Stories: vantage, pivot, lesson points	
Attentive listening—mindful, calm, open, reflective	**Expressing Empathy** • Empathy Reflections: observations, feelings, needs, requests • Celebrate Progress • Clarifying Focus	

Using Evocative Coaching Style Points
(Strengths Building Turn)

Attentive listening—mindful, calm, open, reflective, imaginative	**Appreciative Inquiry** • Discovering Strengths • Observing Vitalities • Framing Aspirations • Inviting Possibilities	
Attentive listening—mindful, calm, open, reflective, imaginative	**Design Thinking** • Brainstorming Ideas • Designing Experiments • Aligning Environments • Confirming Commitment	
	• Session Feedback	

Coaching Style Points

Name:_____Date: _____

Coach:_____Time:_____

Style Point	Notes
Establish rapport	
Celebrate progress	
Explore stories	
Listen attentively	
Offer empathy	
Clarify focus	
Discover strengths	
Explore opportunities	
Frame aspirations	
Identify resources	
Brainstorm ideas	
Design a SMARTER experiment	
Confirm commitment	
Roll with resistance	
Explore culture change	
Seek feedback	

Immunity Map Worksheet

Name:_____Date:_____

Commitment (Improvement goals)	Doing / Not Doing Instead (Behaviors that work against the goals)	Hidden Competing Commitments	Big Assumptions
		Worry Box:	

Adapted from Kegan, R., & Lahey, L. L. (2009). *Immunity to change: How to overcome it and unlock the potential in yourself and your organization.* Boston, MA: Harvard Business School Press.

Charting Talk Time

Coach:_____ Teacher:_____

Date of Conference:_____ Time of Conference:_____

Minute	Teacher	Total	Coach	Total
0:00				
1:00				
2:00				
3:00				
4:00				
5:00				
6:00				
7:00				
8:00				
9:00				
10:00				
11:00				
12:00				
13:00				
14:00				
15:00				
16:00				
17:00				
18:00				
19:00				
20:00				
21:00				
22:00				
23:00				
24:00				
25:00				
26:00				
27:00				
28:00				
29:00				
30:00				
31:00				
32:00				
33:00				
34:00				
35:00				
Total				

Charting Coach Behaviors

Coach: _____   Teacher: _____

Date of Conference: _____   Time of Conference: _____

Time Interval	1. Listening	2. Questioning	3. Presenting	4. Reflecting	5. Clarifying	6. Brainstorming	7. Designing	8. Aligning	9. Celebrating	10. Humor
2										
4										
6										
8										
10										
12										
14										
16										
18										
20										
22										
24										
26										
28										
30										
32										
34										
36										
38										
40										
42										
44										
46										
Total										

Confidential Collaborative Coaching Log

COACHEE: _____

COACH: _____

DATE: _____

Identified Strengths/Areas of Pride	Current Areas of Focus/Challenges
Aspirations	**Progress toward Goals/Experimental Design**
Coachee's Next Steps	**Coach's Next Steps**
Next Meeting Agenda	**Next Meeting Date and Time**

Learning Brief Template

Coachee:_____Coach:_____Date:_____
Presenting Situation (What are the contexts and considerations for our work together? What does the coachee want to focus on?):
Underlying Needs & Values (What is really important to pay attention to, respect, and honor? What does the coachee value most?):
Desired Outcomes (What would improve or even transform this situation for the coachee? What does the coachee want to learn?):
Work Plan (What and how will we work together? Be specific as to the parameters of the coaching relationship.):

References

Csikszentmihalyi, M. (1990). *Flow*. New York, NY: Harper & Row.

Gunn, J. (2020). Why the "A" in STEAM education is just as important as every other letter. Retrieved from https://resilienteducator.com/leaders-link/importance-of-arts-in-steam-education/

Kegan, R., & Lahey, L. L. (2009). *Immunity to change: How to overcome it and unlock potential in yourself and your organization*. Boston, MA: Harvard Business Press.

Palmer, P. (1998). *The courage to teach: Exploring the inner landscape of a teacher's life*. San Francisco, CA: Jossey-Bass.

Roberts, M. (2000). *Horse sense for people*. New York, NY: Putnam.

Tschannen-Moran, M., & Hoy, W. K. (1997). Trust in schools: A conceptual and empirical analysis. *Journal of Educational Administration*, 36(4), 332–354.

Tschannen-Moran, M., & Tschannen-Moran, B. (2018). *Evoking greatness: Coaching to bring out the best in educational leaders*. Thousand Oaks, CA: Corwin.

Tschannen-Moran, M., & Tschannen-Moran, B. (2020). *Evocative coaching: Transforming schools one conversation at a time* (2nd ed.). Thousand Oaks, CA: Corwin.

Index

A SAGE Publishing Company

Helping educators make the greatest impact

CORWIN HAS ONE MISSION: to enhance education through intentional professional learning.

We build long-term relationships with our authors, educators, clients, and associations who partner with us to develop and continuously improve the best evidence-based practices that establish and support lifelong learning.

Solutions YOU WANT | Experts YOU TRUST | Results YOU NEED

EVENTS >>> **INSTITUTES**

Corwin Institutes provide large regional events where educators collaborate with peers and learn from industry experts. Prepare to be recharged and motivated!

corwin.com/institutes

ON-SITE PD >>> **ON-SITE PROFESSIONAL LEARNING**

Corwin on-site PD is delivered through high-energy keynotes, practical workshops, and custom coaching services designed to support knowledge development and implementation.

corwin.com/pd

>>> **PROFESSIONAL DEVELOPMENT RESOURCE CENTER**

The PD Resource Center provides school and district PD facilitators with the tools and resources needed to deliver effective PD.

corwin.com/pdrc

ONLINE >>> **ADVANCE**

Designed for K–12 teachers, Advance offers a range of online learning options that can qualify for graduate-level credit and apply toward license renewal.

corwin.com/advance

Contact a PD Advisor at (800) 831-6640 or visit www.corwin.com for more information